BUGS! BUGS! BUGS!

ACTIVITY BOOK

Tony J. Tallarico

D1502174

Dover Publications
Garden City, New York

You'll find all sorts of bugs—as well as mazes, word searches, letter codes, hidden objects, and scrambled names—in this one-of-a-kind activity book. There's lots of information about the bugs, too. Find out how bombardier beetles react when disturbed, how katydids got their nickname, and why spiders use only the tips of their legs when they build their nests, among other fascinating facts! If you're stumped for an answer, you can turn to the Solutions section, which begins on page 37.

Copyright

Copyright © 2012 by Tony J. Tallarico.
All rights reserved.

Bibliographical Note

Bugs! Bugs! Bugs! Activity Book is a new work, first published by Dover Publications in 2012.

International Standard Book Number

ISBN-13: 978-0-486-48399-3
ISBN-10: 0-486-48399-1

Manufactured in the United States of America
48399108   2023
www.doverpublications.com

A BIG JUMPER

Which one of these four insects can jump the farthest?

Only ONE path will lead to "THE WINNER" circle. Carefully choose the correct one.

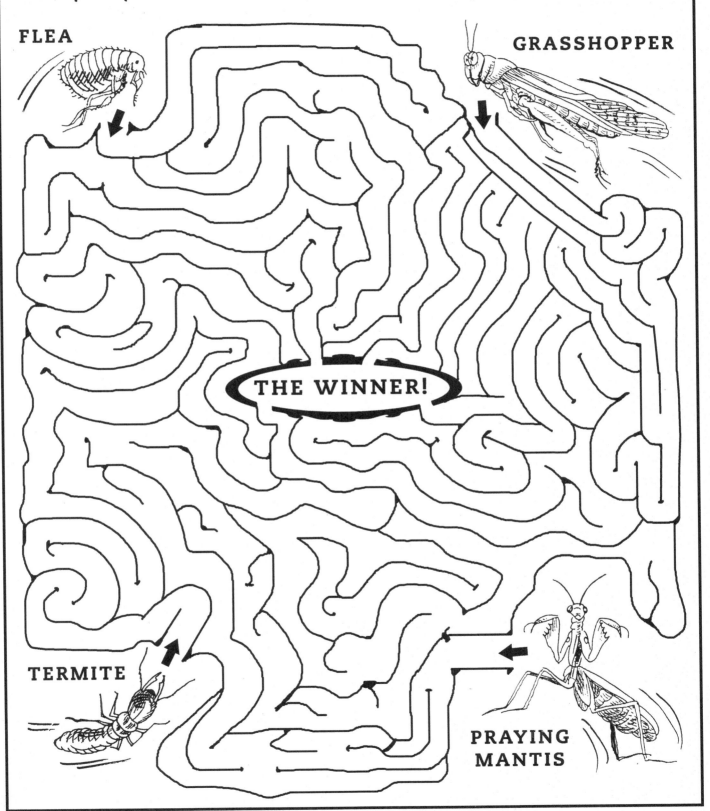

FLEA

GRASSHOPPER

THE WINNER!

TERMITE

PRAYING MANTIS

ARTHROPODS

Arthropods are animals with segmented bodies and six or more jointed legs. They are the largest animal group on Earth and are found in every environment including the ocean. The major groups of arthropods include crustaceans, arachnids, centipedes, millipedes, and of course insects (the most populous species of arthropods).

Find and circle the names of these arthropods in the puzzle below.

☐ANT ☐BEETLE ☐BOLL WEEVIL
☐CENTIPEDE ☐CICADA
☐COCKROACH ☐JUNEBUG
☐MILLIPEDE ☐SCORPION ☐SPIDER

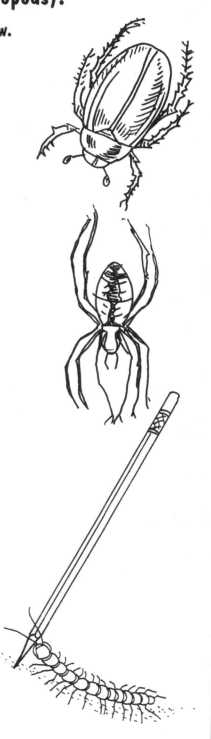

```
M I G U B E N U J
T R E D I P S M B
B N C C U B C I L
E B A O N T O L I
D E O C B O R L V
E B R K R B P I E
P T K R B A I P E
I B C O D B O E W
T V O A B W N D L
N B C C I O N E L
E I T H J G U B O
C E B E L T E E B
```

BEETLEMANIA

Bombardier beetles are ground beetles that typically live in woodlands and grasslands. When disturbed, these beetles can eject a noxious chemical spray from special glands in their abdomen. The ejection has a popping sound!

Find and circle these ten hidden objects in this scene.

☐ BIRD ☐ CAMERA ☐ FISH
☐ FLOWER ☐ HAT ☐ MUSHROOM
☐ PENCIL ☐ RING ☐ SHOE
☐ STAR

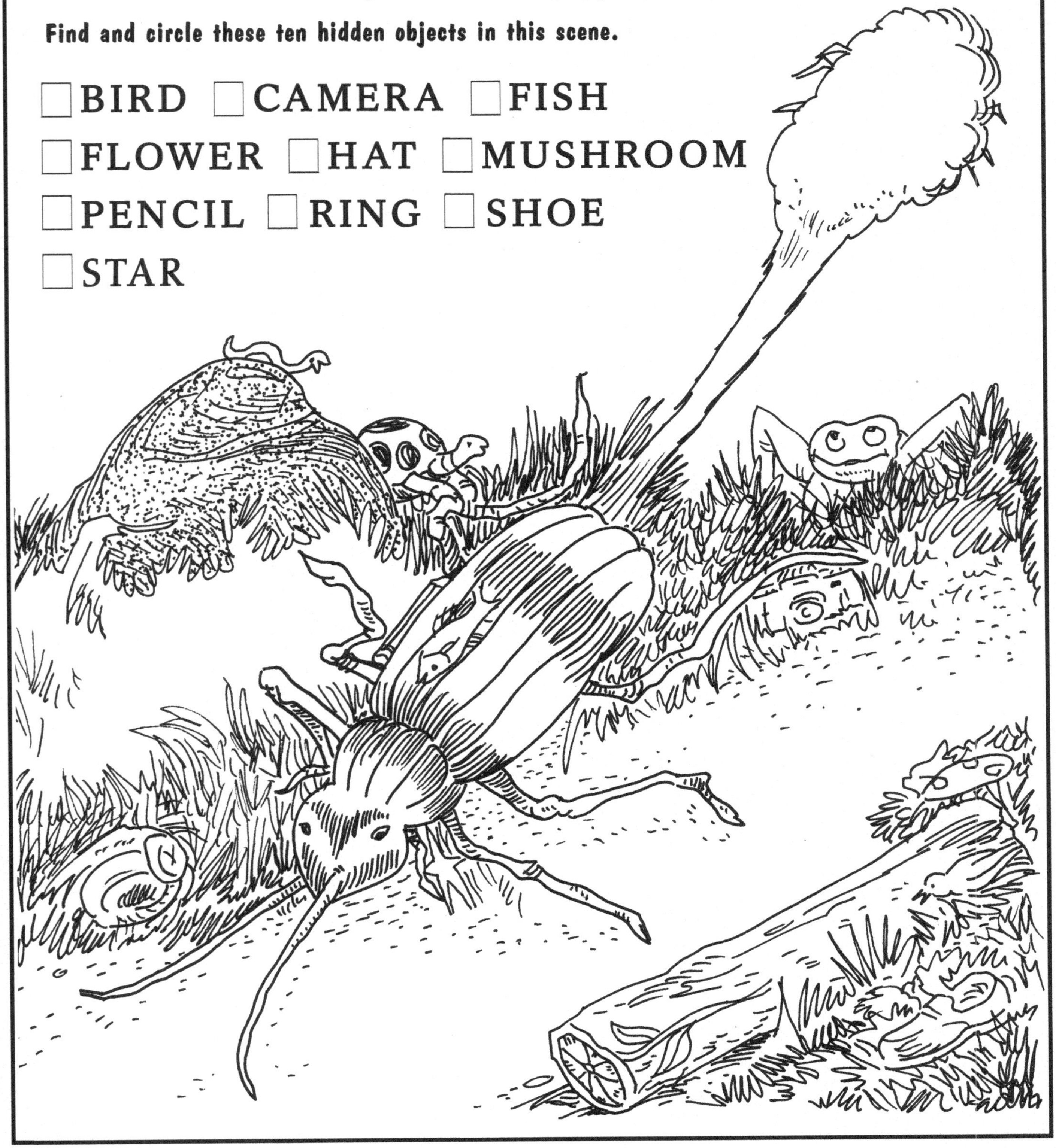

BOLL WEEVILS

Boll weevils are actually beetles that measure just six millimeters long. Despite their size, they have a huge appetite for cotton buds and flowers. First entering the U.S. from Mexico in the late 19th century, boll weevils infested all U.S. cotton-growing areas by the 1920s.

The word COTTON appears 5 times in this puzzle. Find and circle each one. The letters that remain, once listed in the order they appear, will help spell out the fact below.

```
N O T T O C
D E S T R U C O T
C O T T O N I T V
E P E S T N O R T T H
N O T T O C A M O E
R I C C O T T O N A
```

BOLL WEEVILS REMAIN THE MOST COTTON _ _ _ _ _ _ _ _ _ _ IN _ _ _ _ _ _ _ _.

BUTTERFLIES

There are close to 20,000 species of butterflies spread throughout almost the entire world. More than 750 species of them live in the United States and Canada. Antarctica is the only continent on which no butterflies have been found.

How many times does the word BUTTERFLIES appear in this puzzle? Circle and count each one.

```
B S B S
U U B S
B T U U B
B T T U U B
  E T E U U U S
  R E B R U U T
  F R U B F U U T
  L F U B U L U U E
  I L U B U T I U U R B B
  E I U B U T U E U U F E S
  S E U B U R U U S U U L U B
    S E I L F R E T T U B I U
      B U B L U T E R F L U E S
        B U T T E R F L I E S
        E B U L F R S T U B
        S E I L U U L I E S
        S F R E T T U B
```

Total:

_____

CLOTHING MOTH

Tineola bisselliella, otherwise known as Clothing Moth, can be a serious pest. They get their nourishment from clothing, especially wool!

Complete this dot-to-dot picture to discover what this moth has been feeding on.

COCKROACH

An unwelcome household "visitor," the cockroach is actually related to the grasshopper and cricket. Residents of planet Earth for about 250 million years, there are over 3,500 species of them!
What do cockroaches use their antennae or feelers for?

Cross out all the ODD-NUMEBERED letters that appear in the puzzle below. Then write the remaining EVEN-NUMBERED letters, in the order they appear, in the blank spaces to form the answer.

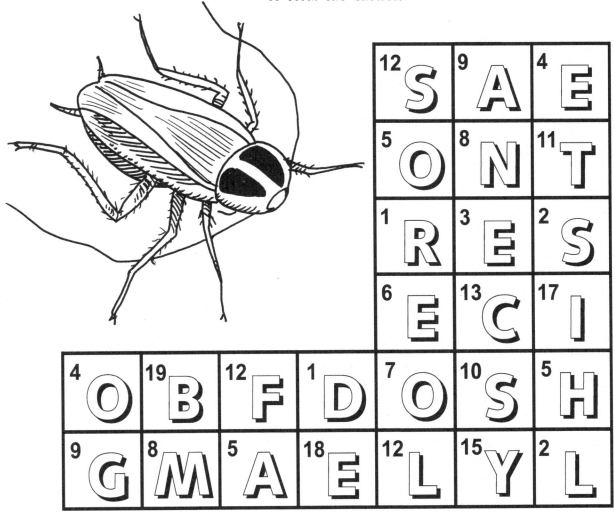

ANSWER:

THEIR FEELERS PROVIDE THEM WITH A

_ _ _ _ _ _ _ _ _ _ _ _ _ .

CRICKETS

Males of most cricket species make a loud chirping sound, which is created when their wings are rubbed together.

Find and circle the following words (having to do with crickets) in the puzzle below. The letters that remain, once listed in the order they appear, will help complete the mystery sentence.

ANTENNAE
CHIRP
COLD-BLOODED
COMMON
INSECT
JUMP
LEAP
LEGS
LOUD
NOCTURNAL
SING
SOUND
WINGS

```
D E D O O L B B D L O C
U G O O D L U C A C K
O J U M P C G O N O U
L N T R I R N E R M T
E S P E O S I P U M C
A L W I N G S H T O E
P E K E E E P A C N S
D N U O S L S A O P N
E T E A N N E T N A I
```

mystery sentence:

CONSIDERED _ _ _ _ _ _ _ _ _ IN

SOME _ _ _ _ _ _ _ _ _ _ , _ _ _ _ _ _

HAVE BEEN KNOWN TO _ _ _ _

THIS INSECT _ _ _ _ _ _ _ !

DEER TICKS

Deer ticks, also known as blacklegged ticks, are just one of many known tick species. They are found in hardwood forests and wooded and brushy areas that are also unfortunately home to deer. Deer ticks are potential carriers of Lyme disease.

Can you find and circle 8 deer, who are all hiding from this deer tick?

DRAGONFLY

The dragonfly is the fastest flier and has the keenest vision of any insect. A dragonfly can hit 60 miles per hour!

Darken in the areas that have a DOT •
to complete this word puzzle.

EYES OF A FLY

Although a fly has very large eyes that cover most of its head, a fly can't pick up as many visual details as human eyes.

There is a benefit though of having very large eyes ... use this chart to decode and complete the fact below.

	A.	B.	C.	D.
1.	S	G	F	O
2.	L	R	Y	H
3.	D	T	C	I
4.	V	E	N	A

I think I see you!

B E C A U S E   __ __ __ __ __   H A V E
                  1C 2A 3D 4B 1A

3 6 0 - __ __ __ __ __ __   __ __ __ __ __ __ '
        3A 4B 1B 2B 4B 4B   4A 3D 1A 3D 1D 4C

T H E Y   C A N   __ __ __
                 1A 4B 4B

__ __ __ __ __ __ __ __   C O M I N G   A T
4D 4C 2C 3B 2D 3D 4C 1B

T H E M .   __ __ __ __   I S   W H Y
          3B 2D 3D 1A   4B 1A

I T   I S   S O   __ __ __ __   __ __
                  2D 4D 2B 3A   3B 1D

__ __ __ __ __   A   __ __ __ !
3C 4D 3B 3C 2D   1C 2A 2C

GRASSHOPPERS

Although there are between 11,000 and 18,000 different species of grasshoppers in existence, they all have something in common - no ears and five eyes!

Find and circle **12** things that are different between these two grasshopper scenes.

Grasshoppers like to eat grasses, leaves and cereal crops. Some will eat from a single plant, while others will eat from a variety of sources throughout the day.

FLEAS

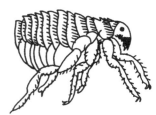

Unwelcome guests of cats and dogs, fleas are wingless insects with mouthparts made for piercing skin and sucking blood.

Complete this dot-to-dot picture.

GROUP OF INSECTS

What is a group of insects called?

Find and circle these 10 words (having to do with insects) in this puzzle.
The letters that remain, once written in the spaces below in the order they appear,
will spell out the answer.

ANTENNAE
BUG
COCOON
COLONIES
CRAWL
LARVA
MOLT
NEST
POLLEN
WINGS

E	A	N	N	E	T	N	A
S	E	I	N	O	L	O	C
G	T	A	E	S	A	L	O
N	L	W	S	G	R	W	C
I	O	A	T	U	V	A	O
W	M	R	M	B	A	R	O
N	E	L	L	O	P	C	N

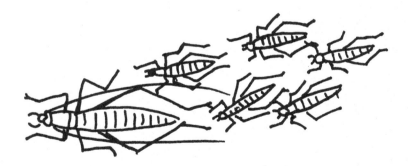

A GROUP OF INSECTS IS CALLED

___   ___ ___ ___ ___

HERCULES BEETLE

The Hercules beetle's name is well deserved as males can reach 6.75 inches in length! Where is this giant bug found?

Choose the correct path to discover the answer.

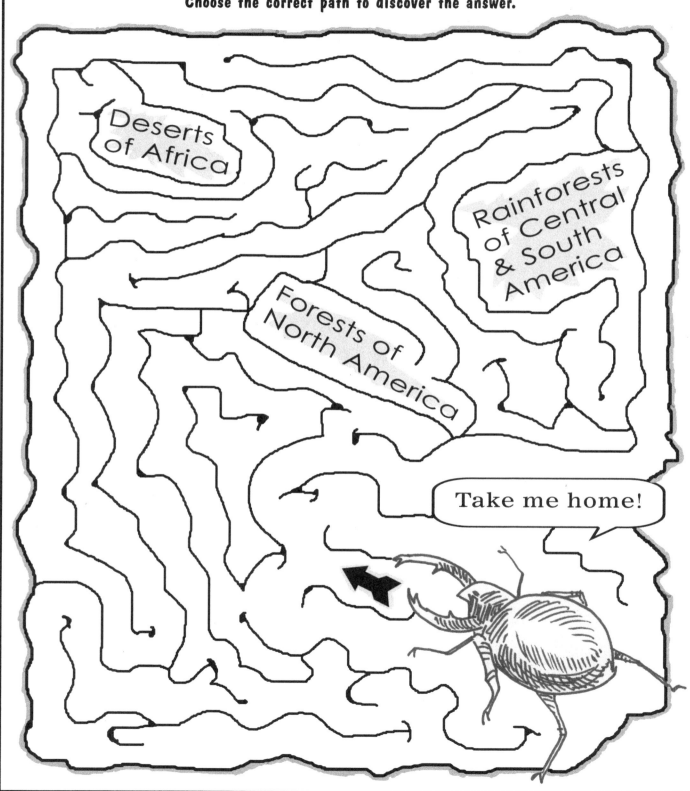

HOUSE FLIES

House flies are the most common of all domestic flies and are one of the most widely distributed insects, found all over the world. Considered pests, they are active only in daytime and rest at night.

How many flies can you find in this scene? Circle and count each one.

TOTAL: ___

HOW MANY INSECTS?

How many different kinds of insects are there? It seems like an impossible question for good reason - we don't even know how many different insect species there are in the world!

Fill in the areas that have a letter from the word **INSECT** (with a dark pencil) to complete the sentence below.

SCIENTISTS ESTIMATE THAT THERE ARE BETWEEN

AND

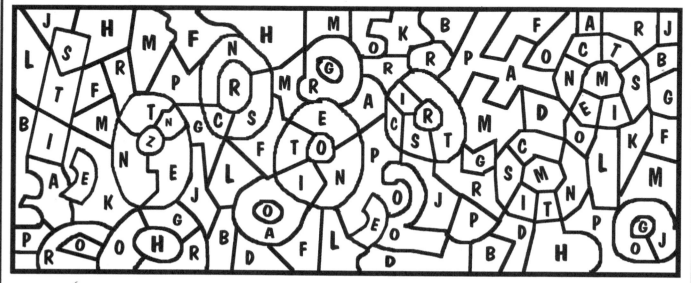

SPECIES OF INSECTS IN THE WORLD.

HUNGRY BATS

Although they may seem scary, bats are harmless but play an important role in combating insects that are actually dangerous to humans. Did you know that pesty mosquitoes make up a significant portion of a bat's diet?

How many mosquitoes can a bat consume in just one hour? Fill in the areas that contain a dark circle ● to reveal the answer.

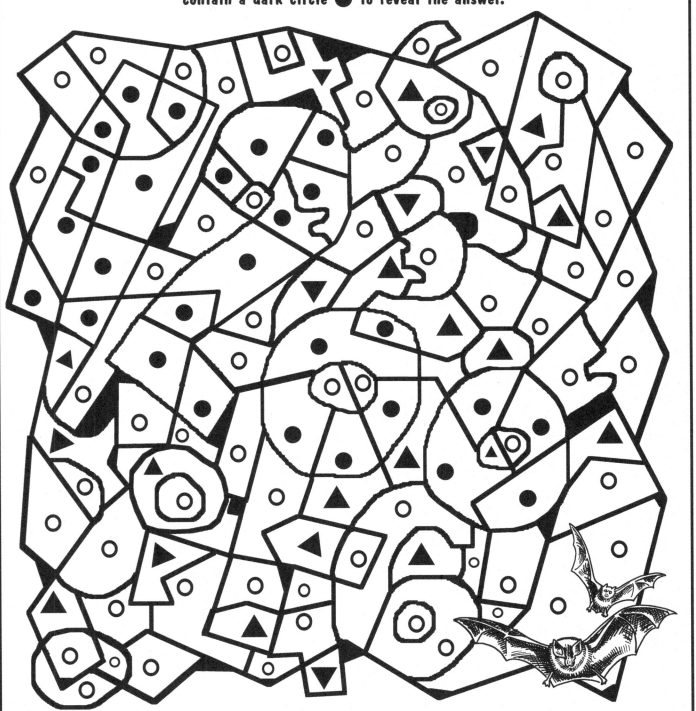

"KATY DID"

Katydids are large, singing, winged insects. Males have song-producing, or stridulating, organs on their front wings. Females respond to the shrill song of the males with a sound that sort of mimics "katy did, katy didn't," hence the name!

These five Katydids may appear the same ... but look closely as only 2 are identical. Find and circle them.

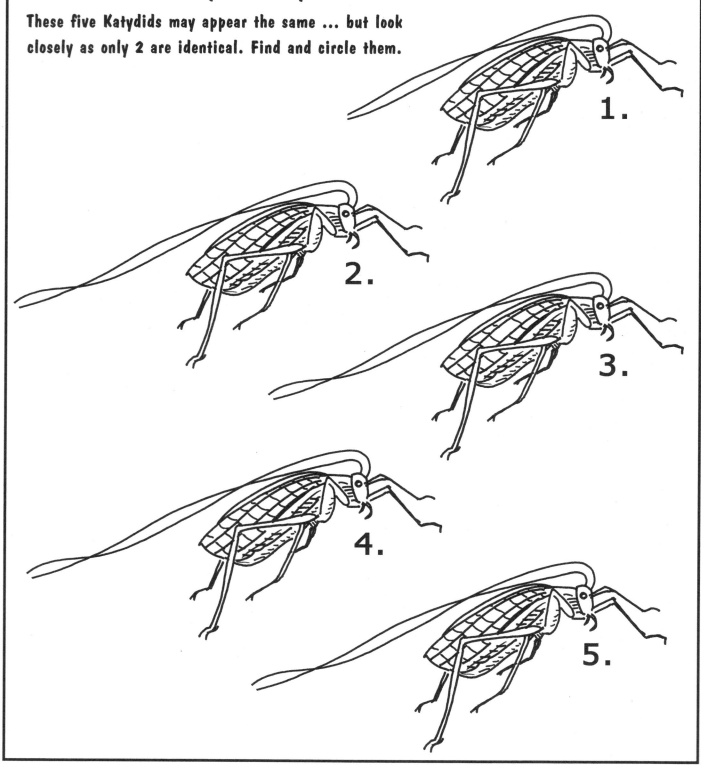

LARGEST GROUP

The firefly, lady beetle and stag beetle are just three of the more than 360,000 species that make up the largest order in the animal kingdom. This group includes 40% of all insects and nearly 30% of all animal species.

Use the chart below to decode the scientific name of this group of species.

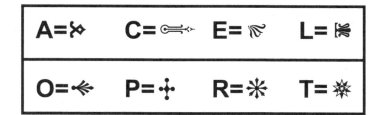

A=✗	C=☞	E=☞	L=✦
O=«	P=✛	R=✳	T=✴

You know me as a firefly, but I'm actually a beetle!

I'm a lady beetle, more commonly know as a ladybug!

I'm called a Stag beetle because of the antlers found on my head.

MORE REBUS FUN

These rebuses are letter-and-picture puzzles that spell out names of insects.

Decode each rebus puzzle and write the name of each insect in the blank spaces.

_ _ _ _ _ _ _

_ _ _ _ _ _ _ _ _

NAME THIS BUG

This bug, only about 1/5 inch long, loves to feed on grass plants. They are known for damaging most home lawns and golf courses!

Write the opposite of each word. One letter from every word will help spell out the name of this turf-loving bug.

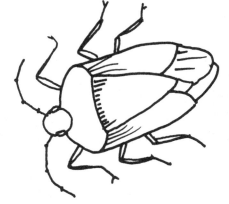

HOT ⟶ __ __ __ __

DULL ⟶ __ __ I __ __

STAND ⟶ __ __ __

OLD ⟶ __ __ __

FAR ⟶ __ L __ __ __ __

TALL ⟶ __ __ R __

TOP ⟶ __ __ T __ __ __

CLOUDY ⟶ __ __ __ __ Y

WRONG ⟶ __ __ __ H __

PICTURE CLUES

Complete the names of these insects by using each of the picture clues.

_ _ _ _ _   S P I D E R

_ _ _ _ _   F L Y

_ _ _ _ _ _ _   C R I C K E T

_ _ _ _   W I G

REBUS FUN

These rebuses are letter-and-picture puzzles that spell out names of insects.

Decode each rebus puzzle and write the name of each insect in the blank spaces.

_ _ _ _ _ _ _

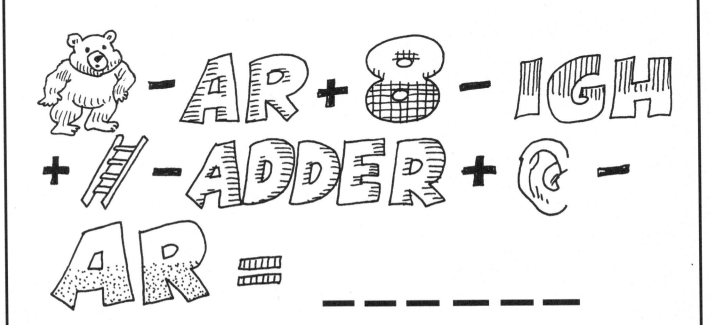

_ _ _ _ _ _ _

SCRAMBLED BUG NAMES

Unscramble the names of these bugs and write them in their spaces.
(The written clues and pictures will help!)

"Related to a butterfly, I'm attracted to light."

T M H O

_ _ _ _

"I make dogs itch."

A L E F

_ _ _ _

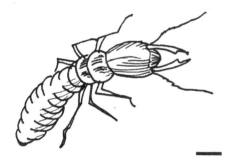

"I love to eat wood."

M E R T E I T

_ _ _ _ _ _ _

"Farmers love me because I eat plant-eating insects."

B L U A G Y D

_ _ _ _ _ _ _

SILKWORMS

Silkworms (offspring of moths) produce silk by spewing out thread from tiny holes in their jaws, which they use to spin into their egg-bearing cocoons. The entire production takes only 72 hours!

These six silkworms may appear the same ... but look closely as only TWO are identical. Find and circle the TWO that are the same.

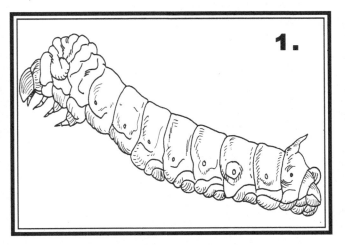

1.

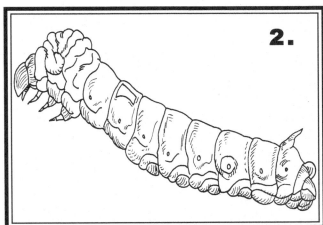

2.

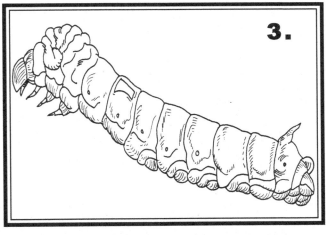

3.

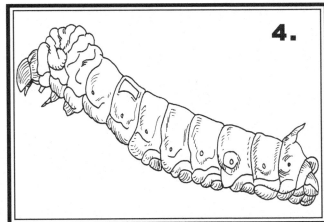

4.

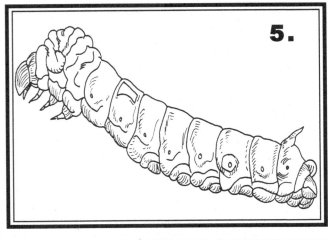

5.

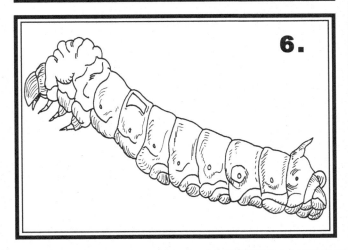

6.

SLUGS

Slugs are basically snails without shells. Having soft and slimy bodies, slugs like moist and damp environments.

How many times does the word SLUGS appear below? Circle and count each one.

```
        S  G  U  L  S
     S  G  U  B  E  N  S
     S  R  U  D  I  P  S  M  S
     B  N  L  C  U  B  C  I  L
  S  E  B  S  O  N  T  O  L  I  S
  G  D  E  O  C  B  O  R  L  V  G
  S  L  U  G  S           I  E  U
  U  P  T           S  P  E  L
  B  I  B  C  O  D  B  O  E  W  S
  S  S  G  U  L  S  W  N  D  S  S
     U  B  C  C  I  O  N  G  G
     S  I  T  H  J  G  U  B  S
        E  B  E  L  L  E  E
        S  U  S  E  S
```

TOTAL: ____

28

STUDY OF INSECTS

Scientists who study insects can have professional careers in many fields. Their jobs may include conducting research, teaching, or even aiding in criminal investigations.

What is the name given to scientists who study insects? Write the name of each picture in the correct spaces. One letter from each will help spell out the answer.

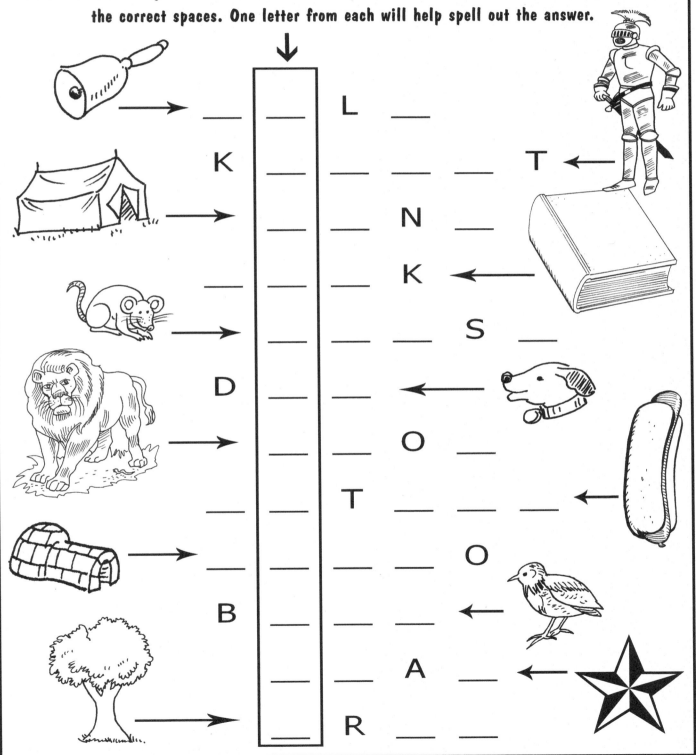

SUMMER BUGS

The beginning of summer is usually marked by the arrival of two noisy and clumsy beetles. Crashing into the side of your home and outdoor lights during uncontrolled flights on hot summer days and nights, these beetles are known by two different names.

Answer each clue correctly. Then write the numbered letters in their correct spaces at the bottom of the page to form the names of these beetles.

NOT FULL __ __ __ __ __
          4   9

SAFE PLACE FOR BIRD'S EGGS __ __ __ __
                            3   14   8

INDEPENDENCE DAY __ __ __ __ __ O F __ __ __ __
                     2   15   1   6   16 11

8TH MONTH OF THE YEAR __ __ __ __ __ __
                       10   7   18

SHORELINE OF AN OCEAN __ __ __ __ __
                       5   13

PLAYED ON DIAMOND-SHAPED FIELD __ __ __ __ __ __ __ __
                                12   17

__ __ __ __   __ __ __ __
1   2   3   4   5   6   7   8

__ __ __   __ __ __ __ __ __ __
9   10 11   12 13 14 15 16 17 18

TARANTULA

A tarantula is actually a large hairy spider whose bite is no more dangerous (to most people) than the sting of a bee. Did you know there is an Italian folk dance named after this creepy crawler?

Write these words in alphabetical order into the puzzle grid.
The third letter of each word will help spell out the name of this upbeat-tempo dance.

TRAIN

ROLE

ATTRACT

MOTH

BLANKET

SALAD

CARRY

HONEY

DRAG

PRESS

THE PAINTED LADY

The Painted Lady is a large butterfly with black-spotted wings. It may be the most widespread butterfly in the world as it can be found in North and South America, Europe, Asia and Africa.

Find and circle the TWO Painted Lady Butterflies that are different from the rest.

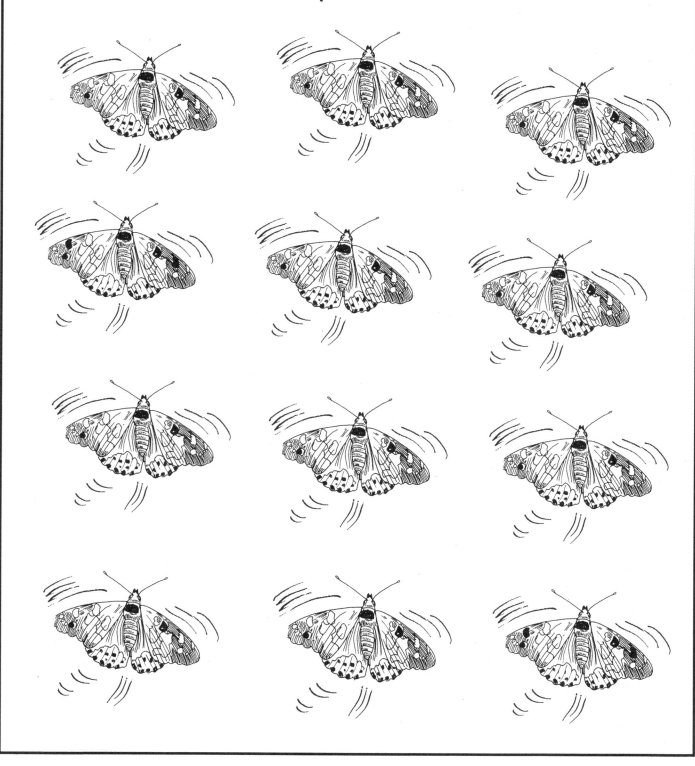

TRAP-DOOR SPIDER

Large, hairy, but harmless, the trap-door spider is a tropical creature that nests underground. This spider makes long burrows in the earth, lines them with silk (which they spin) and fashions the entrance with a bevel-edged, hinged, accurately fitting trapdoor.

Choose the correct path that will lead this insect to the trap-door spider!

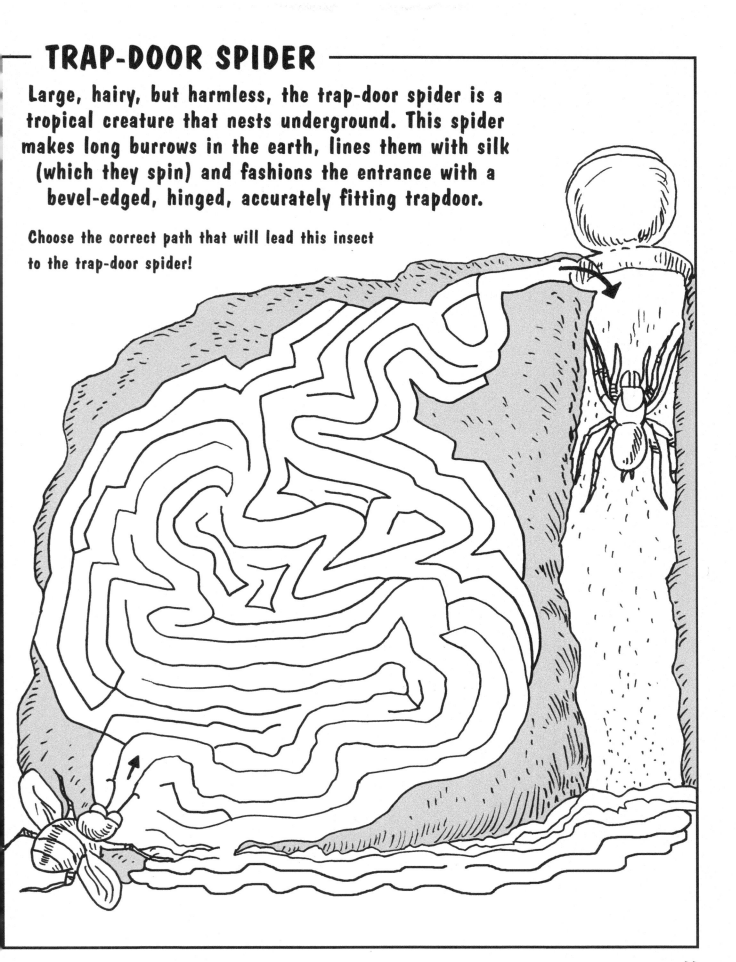

TWIN BEES

Although sometimes mistaken as a wasp or yellowjacket, the bee is a flying insect known for its role in pollination and making honey and beeswax.

Only 2 of these bees have identical twins on this page.

Find the 2 matching pairs and draw lines between them.

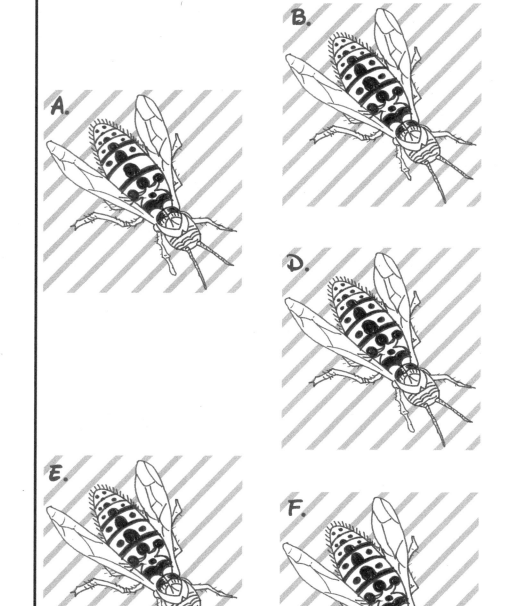
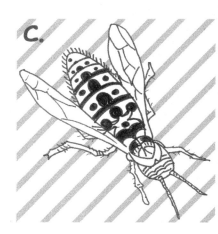
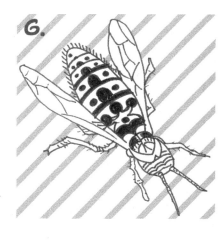

WEB OF KNOWLEDGE

A spider's web is made of silk, which makes the spider the only creature to use silk in its daily life.

To complete the fact below, first circle all the letters that contain a STAR ☆.
Then list these letters in the order they appear, filling in the blanks to form the fact.

SPIDERS _ _ _ _ USE THE _ _ _ _

OF THEIR _ _ _ _ WHEN BUILDING

WEBS SO THAT THEY DON'T GET

_ _ _ _ _ IN

THEIR OWN

_ _ _ _ _ _ _ _ !

WORDS IN A WORD

How many words (with at least 3 letters) can you create using only the letters found in the word **INSECTS**?
Write them below.

Solutions

A BIG JUMPER

Which one of these four insects can jump the furthest?

Only ONE path will lead to "THE WINNER" circle. Carefully choose the correct one.

FLEA

GRASSHOPPER

THE WINNER!

TERMITE

PRAYING MANTIS

Page 1

ARTHROPODS

Arthropods are animals with segmented bodies and six or more jointed legs. They are the largest animal group on Earth and are found in every environment including the ocean. The major groups of arthropods include crustaceans, arachnids, centipedes, millipedes, and of course insects (the most populous species of arthropods).

Find and circle the names of these arthropods in the puzzle below.

☐ANT ☐BEETLE ☐BOLL WEEVIL
☐CENTIPEDE ☐CICADA
☐COCKROACH ☐JUNEBUG
☐MILLIPEDE ☐SCORPION ☐SPIDER

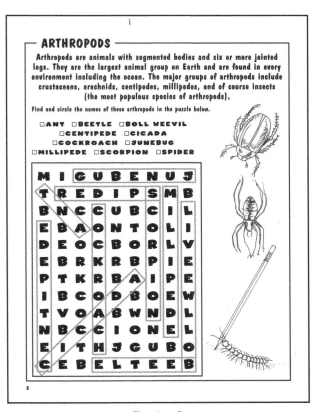

M I G U B E N U J
T R E D I P S M B
B N C C U B C I L
E B A O N T O L I
D E O C B O R L V
E B R K R B P I E
P T K R B A I P E
I B C O D B O E W
T V O A B W N D L
N B C C I O N E L
E I T H J G U B O
C E B E L T E E B

Page 2

BEETLEMANIA

Bombardier beetles are ground beetles that typically live in woodlands and grasslands. When disturbed, these beetles can eject a noxious chemical spray from special glands in their abdomen. The ejection has a popping sound!

Find and circle these ten hidden objects in this scene.

☐BIRD ☐CAMERA ☐FISH
☐FLOWER ☐HAT ☐MUSHROOM
☐PENCIL ☐RING ☐SHOE
☐STAR

Page 3

BOLL WEEVILS

Boll weevils are actually beetles that measure just six millimeters long. Despite their size, they have a huge appetite for cotton buds and flowers. First entering the U.S. from Mexico in the late 19th century, boll weevils infested all U.S. cotton-growing areas by the 1920s.

The word COTTON appears 5 times in this puzzle. Find and circle each one. The letters that remain, once listed in the order they appear, will help spell out the fact below.

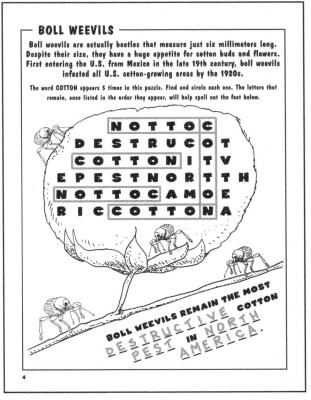

N O T T O C
D E S T R U C O T
C O T T O N I T V
E P E S T N O R T T H
N O T T O C A M O E
R I C C O T T O N A

BOLL WEEVILS REMAIN THE MOST DESTRUCTIVE COTTON PEST IN NORTH AMERICA.

Page 4

Solutions

BUTTERFLIES

There are close to 20,000 species of butterflies spread throughout almost the entire world. More than 750 species of them live in the United States and Canada. Antarctica is the only continent on which no butterflies have been found.

How many times does the word BUTTERFLIES appear in this puzzle? Circle and count each one.

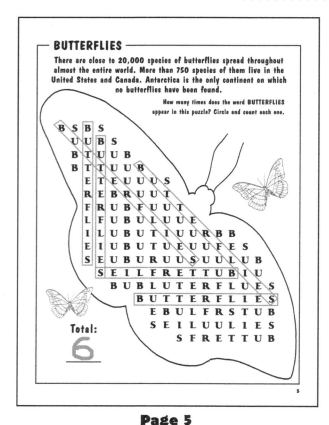

Total: **6**

Page 5

CLOTHING MOTH

Tineola bisselliella, otherwise known as Clothing Moth, can be a serious pest. They get their nourishment from clothing, especially wool!

Complete this dot-to-dot picture to discover what this moth has been feeding on.

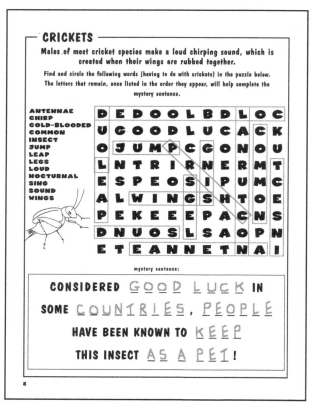

THANKS FOR THE SNACK!

Page 6

COCKROACH

An unwelcome household "visitor," the cockroach is actually related to the grasshopper and cricket. Residents of planet Earth for about 250 million years, there are over 3,500 species of them! What do cockroaches use their antennae or feelers for?

Cross out all the ODD-NUMBERED letters that appear in the puzzle below. Then write the remaining EVEN-NUMBERED letters, in the order they appear, in the blank spaces to form the answer.

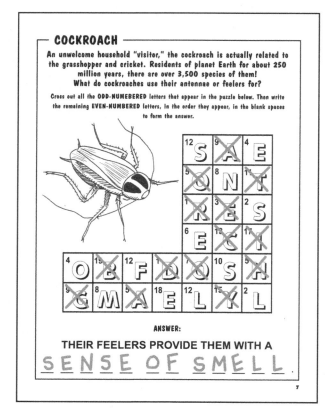

ANSWER:

THEIR FEELERS PROVIDE THEM WITH A

SENSE OF SMELL.

Page 7

CRICKETS

Males of most cricket species make a loud chirping sound, which is created when their wings are rubbed together.

Find and circle the following words (having to do with crickets) in the puzzle below. The letters that remain, once listed in the order they appear, will help complete the mystery sentence.

ANTENNAE
CHIRP
COLD-BLOODED
COMMON
INSECT
JUMP
LEAP
LEGS
LOUD
NOCTURNAL
SING
SOUND
WINGS

```
D E D O O L B D L O C
U G O O D L U C A C K
O J U M P C G O N O U
L N T R I R N E R M T
E S P E O S I P U M C
A L W I N G S H T O E
P E K E E E P A C N S
D N U O S L S A O P N
E T E A N N E T N A I
```

mystery sentence:

CONSIDERED GOOD LUCK IN

SOME COUNTRIES, PEOPLE

HAVE BEEN KNOWN TO KEEP

THIS INSECT AS A PET!

Page 8

Solutions

DEER TICKS

Deer ticks, also known as blacklegged ticks, are just one of many known tick species. They are found in hardwood forests and wooded and brushy areas that are also unfortunately home to deer. Deer ticks are potential carriers of Lyme disease.

Can you find and circle 8 deer, who are all hiding from this deer tick?

Page 9

DRAGONFLY

The dragonfly is the fastest flier and has the keenest vision of any insect. A dragonfly can hit 60 miles per hour!

Darken in the areas that have a DOT • to complete this word puzzle.

Page 10

EYES OF A FLY

Although a fly has very large eyes that cover most of its head, a fly can't pick up as many visual details as human eyes.

There is a benefit though of having very large eyes ... use this chart to decode and complete the fact below.

	A.	B.	C.	D.
1.	S	G	F	O
2.	L	R	Y	H
3.	D	T	C	I
4.	V	E	N	A

I think I see you!

BECAUSE F L I E S HAVE
         1C 2A 3D 4B 1A

360- D E G R E E   V I S I O N,
     3A 4B 1B 2B 4B 4B   4A 3D 1A 3D 1D 4C

THEY CAN S E E
           1A 4B 4B

A N Y T H I N G COMING AT
4D 4C 2C 3B 2D 3D 4C 1B

THEM. T H I S IS WHY
       3B 2D 3D 1A   4B 1A

IT IS SO H A R D T O
            2D 1B 2B 3A   3B 1D

C A T C H A F L Y !
3C 4D 3B 3C 2D   1C 2A 2C

Page 11

GRASSHOPPERS

Although there are between 11,000 and 18,000 different species of grasshoppers in existence, they all have something in common - no ears and five eyes!

Find and circle 12 things that are different between these two grasshopper scenes.

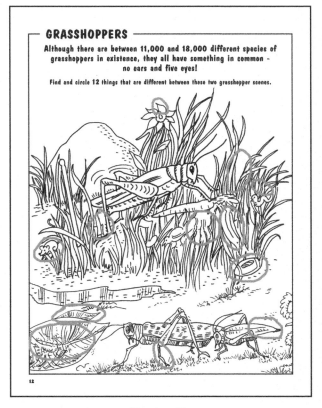

Page 12

Solutions

Grasshoppers like to eat grasses, leaves and cereal crops. Some will eat from a single plant, while others will eat from a variety of sources throughout the day.

13

Page 13

FLEAS

Unwelcome guests of cats and dogs, fleas are wingless insects with mouthparts made for piercing skin and sucking blood.

Complete this dot-to-dot picture.

I'm a cartoon flea!

I'm a cartoon dog!

14

Page 14

GROUP OF INSECTS

What is a group of insects called?

Find and circle these 10 words (having to do with insects) in this puzzle.
The letters that remain, once written in the spaces below in the order they appear, will spell out the answer.

ANTENNAE
BUG
COCOON
COLONIES
CRAWL
LARVA
MOLT
NEST
POLLEN
WINGS

E	A	N	N	E	T	N	A
S	E	I	N	O	L	O	C
G	T	A	E	S	A	L	O
N	L	W	S	G	R	W	C
I	O	A	T	U	V	A	O
W	M	R	M	B	A	R	O
N	E	L	L	O	P	C	N

A GROUP OF INSECTS IS CALLED

A SWARM

15

Page 15

HERCULES BEETLE

The Hercules beetle's name is well deserved as males can reach 6.75 inches in length! Where is this giant bug found?

Choose the correct path to discover the answer.

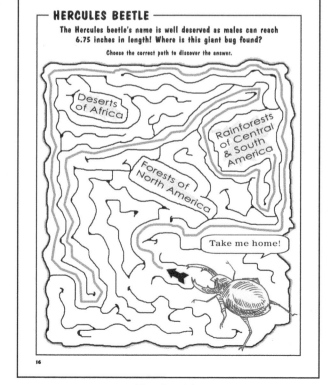

Deserts of Africa

Rainforests of Central & South America

Forests of North America

Take me home!

16

Page 16

Solutions

HOUSE FLIES

House flies are the most common of all domestic flies and are one of the most widely distributed insects, found all over the world. Considered pests, they are active only in daytime and rest at night.

How many flies can you find in this scene? Circle and count each one.

TOTAL: 10

Page 17

HOW MANY INSECTS?

How many different kinds of insects are there? It seems like an impossible question for good reason - we don't even know how many different insect species there are in the world!

Fill in the areas that have a letter from the word INSECT (with a dark pencil) to complete the sentence below.

SCIENTISTS ESTIMATE THAT THERE ARE BETWEEN

AND

SPECIES OF INSECTS IN THE WORLD.

Page 18

HUNGRY BATS

Although they may seem scary, bats are harmless but play an important role in combating insects that are actually dangerous to humans. Did you know that pesty mosquitoes make up a significant portion of a bat's diet?

How many mosquitoes can a bat consume in just one hour? Fill in the areas that contain a dark circle ● to reveal the answer.

Page 19

"KATY DID"

Katydids are large, singing, winged insects. Males have song-producing, or stridulating, organs on their front wings. Females respond to the shrill song of the males with a sound that sort of mimics "katy did, katy didn't," hence the name!

These five Katydids may appear the same ... but look closely as only 2 are identical. Find and circle them.

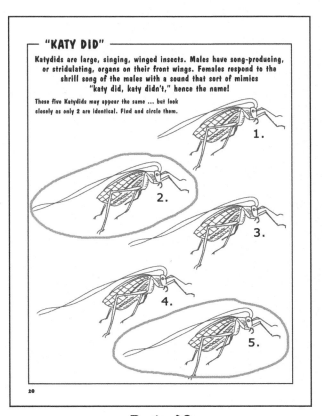

Page 20

Solutions

LARGEST GROUP

The firefly, lady beetle and stag beetle are just three of the more than 360,000 species that make up the largest order in the animal kingdom. This group includes 40% of all insects and nearly 30% of all animal species.

Use the chart below to decode the scientific name of this group of species.

A=⋈	C=⊶	E=☞	L=✾
O=⬅	P=✝	R=✳	T=✳

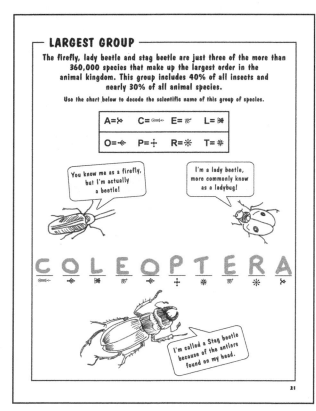

You know me as a firefly, but I'm actually a beetle!

I'm a lady beetle, more commonly know as a ladybug!

C O L E O P T E R A

I'm called a Stag beetle because of the antlers found on my head.

Page 21

MORE REBUS FUN

These rebuses are letter-and-picture puzzles that spell out names of insects.

Decode each rebus puzzle and write the name of each insect in the blank spaces.

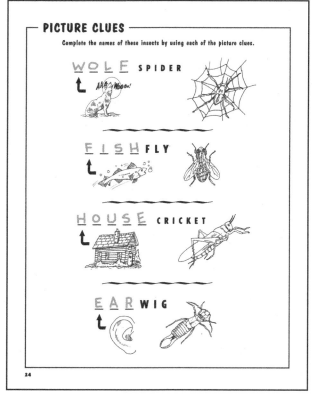

☆ - TAR + 🧁 - E + 🥁 - RUM + 👁 - YE + 🚗 - CA =

S P I D E R

1⊘ - N + 💍 - ING + 👦 - ASK + 🎪 - NT =

T E R M I T E

Page 22

NAME THIS BUG

This bug, only about 1/5 inch long, loves to feed on grass plants. They are known for damaging most home lawns and golf courses!

Write the opposite of each word. One letter from every word will help spell out the name of this turf-loving bug.

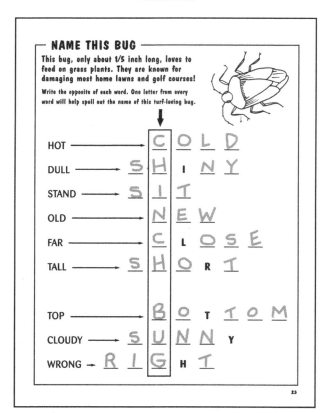

HOT	→	C O L D
DULL	→	S H I N Y
STAND	→	S I T
OLD	→	N E W
FAR	→	C L O S E
TALL	→	S H O R T
TOP	→	B O T T O M
CLOUDY	→	S U N N Y
WRONG	→	R I G H T

Page 23

PICTURE CLUES

Complete the names of these insects by using each of the picture clues.

W O L F SPIDER

F I S H FLY

H O U S E CRICKET

E A R WIG

Page 24

Solutions

REBUS FUN

These rebuses are letter-and-picture puzzles that spell out names of insects.

Decode each rebus puzzle and write the name of each insect in the blank spaces.

－SH＋／－AK
＋4－OUR＋👄
－IPS＋🪀－OYO
＝ F I R E F L Y

－AR＋8－IGH
＋📏－ADDER＋👂－
AR＝ B E E T L E

Page 25

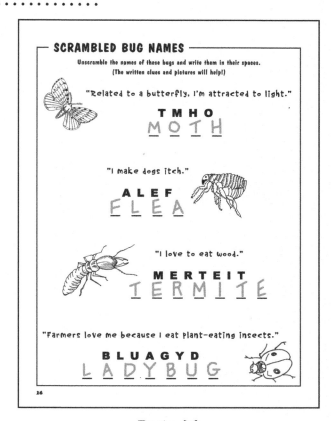

SCRAMBLED BUG NAMES

Unscramble the names of these bugs and write them in their spaces.
(The written clues and pictures will help!)

"Related to a butterfly, I'm attracted to light."

T M H O
M O T H

"I make dogs itch."

A L E F
F L E A

"I love to eat wood."

M E R T E I T
T E R M I T E

"Farmers love me because I eat plant-eating insects."

B L U A G Y D
L A D Y B U G

Page 26

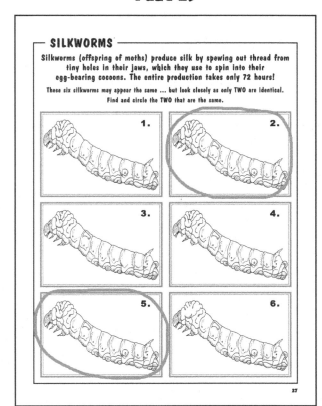

SILKWORMS

Silkworms (offspring of moths) produce silk by spewing out thread from tiny holes in their jaws, which they use to spin into their egg-bearing cocoons. The entire production takes only 72 hours!

These six silkworms may appear the same ... but look closely as only TWO are identical.
Find and circle the TWO that are the same.

1. 2. 3. 4. 5. 6.

Page 27

SLUGS

Slugs are basically snails without shells. Having soft and slimy bodies, slugs like moist and damp environments.

How many times does the word SLUGS appear below? Circle and count each one.

S G U L S
S G U B E N S
S R U D I P S M S
B N L C U B C I L
S E B S O N T O L I S
G D E O C B O R L V G
S L U G S   I E U
U P T   S P E L
B I B C O D B O E W S
S S G U L S W N D S
U B C C I O N G G
S I T H J G U B S
E B E L L E E
S U S E S

TOTAL: 6

Page 28

43

Solutions

STUDY OF INSECTS

Scientists who study insects can have professional careers in many fields. Their jobs may include conducting research, teaching, or even aiding in criminal investigations.

What is the name given to scientists who study insects? Write the name of each picture in the correct spaces. One letter from each will help spell out the answer.

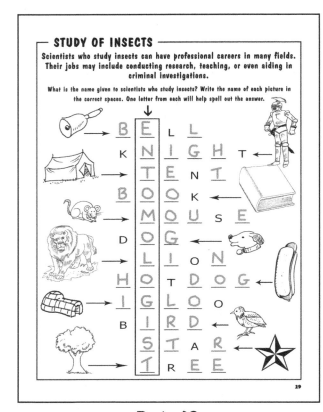

B E L L
K N I G H T T
E N T
B O O K
O M O U S E
D O L I O N
H O T D O G
I G L O O
B I R D
S T A R
T R E E

ENTOMOLOGIST

Page 29

SUMMER BUGS

The beginning of summer is usually marked by the arrival of two noisy and clumsy beetles. Crashing into the side of your home and outdoor lights during uncontrolled flights on hot summer days and nights, these beetles are known by two different names.

Answer each clue correctly. Then write the numbered letters in their correct spaces at the bottom of the page to form the names of these beetles.

| NOT FULL | E M P T Y |
| | 4   9 |

| SAFE PLACE FOR BIRD'S EGGS | N E S T |
| | 3 14 8 |

| INDEPENDENCE DAY | F O U R T H OF J U L Y |
| | 2 15   1 6 16 11 |

| 8TH MONTH OF THE YEAR | A U G U S T |
| | 10   7   18 |

| SHORELINE OF AN OCEAN | B E A C H |
| | 5 13 |

| PLAYED ON DIAMOND-SHAPED FIELD | B A S E B A L L |
| | 12   17 |

J U N E   B U G S
1 2 3 4   5 6 7 8
M A Y   B E E T L E S
9 10 11   12 13 14 15 16 17 18

Page 30

TARANTULA

A tarantula is actually a large hairy spider whose bite is no more dangerous (to most people) than the sting of a bee. Did you know there is an Italian folk dance named after this creepy crawler?

Write these words in alphabetical order into the puzzle grid. The third letter of each word will help spell out the name of this upbeat-tempo dance.

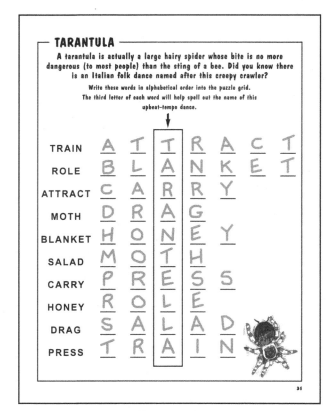

TRAIN	A T T R A C T
ROLE	B L A N K E T
ATTRACT	C A R R Y
MOTH	D R A G
BLANKET	H O N E Y
SALAD	M O R E
CARRY	P R O S E
HONEY	R O A S
DRAG	S A L A D
PRESS	T R A I N

TARANTELLA

Page 31

THE PAINTED LADY

The Painted Lady is a large butterfly with black-spotted wings. It may be the most widespread butterfly in the world as it can be found in North and South America, Europe, Asia and Africa.

Find and circle the TWO Painted Lady Butterflies that are different from the rest.

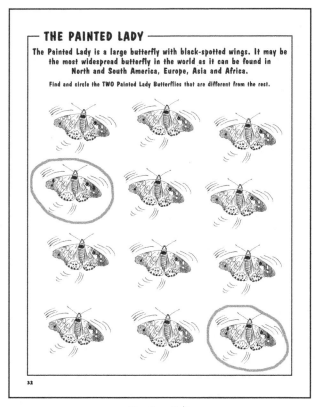

Page 32

44

Solutions

TRAP-DOOR SPIDER

Large, hairy, but harmless, the trap-door spider is a tropical creature that nests underground. This spider makes long burrows in the earth, lines them with silk (which they spin) and fashions the entrance with a bevel-edged, hinged, accurately fitting trapdoor.

Choose the correct path that will lead this insect to the trap-door spider!

33

Page 33

TWIN BEES

Although sometimes mistaken as a wasp or yellowjacket, the bee is a flying insect known for its role in pollination and making honey and beeswax.

Only 2 of these bees have identical twins on this page.
Find the 2 matching pairs and draw lines between them.

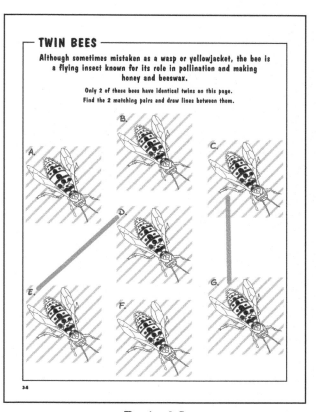

34

Page 34

WEB OF KNOWLEDGE

A spider's web is made of silk, which makes the spider the only creature to use silk in its daily life.

To complete the fact below, first circle all the letters that contain a STAR ☆.
Then list these letters in the order they appear, filling in the blanks to form the fact.

SPIDERS <u>ONLY</u> USE THE <u>TIPS</u>

OF THEIR <u>LEGS</u> WHEN BUILDING

WEBS SO THAT THEY DON'T GET

<u>STUCK</u> IN

THEIR OWN

<u>CREATION</u>!

35

Page 35

WORDS IN A WORD

How many words (with at least 3 letters) can you create using only the letters found in the word **INSECTS**?
Write them below.

Here are 24 of the most common words:

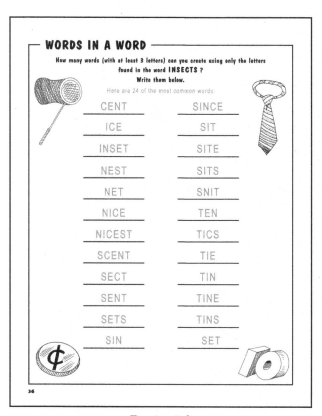

CENT	SINCE
ICE	SIT
INSET	SITE
NEST	SITS
NET	SNIT
NICE	TEN
NICEST	TICS
SCENT	TIE
SECT	TIN
SENT	TINE
SETS	TINS
SIN	SET

36

Page 36